A *Life* with *Purpose* and *Inner* *Quality*

Boca Raton, FL USA
2020

A Life with Purpose and Inner Quality

DONG YU LAN

Copyrights © 2020 by Bookafé

ISBN: 978-1-951159-30-6

Translated from the Brazilian Portuguese:
Original title: *Uma vida de propóstio e qualidade interior*

1st English Edition - August 2017

2nd English Edition - August 2020

All rights reserved by Bookafé

Full or partial reproduction of this book is prohibited without written authorization of its editors.

Published in USA by
Bookafé
PO Box 880096
Boca Raton, FL 33488   USA
Fone: (754) 207-4554
www.lifeforallministry.org

For additional volumes, please order online. See your options on our website:
www.lifeforallministry.org

All scripture quotations, unless otherwise indicated, are taken from the New King James Version®. Copyright ©1982 by Thomas Nelson, Inc. Used by permission. All rights reserved.

Printed in the United States of America
by Bookafé

A Life with Purpose and Inner Quality

Dong Yu Lan

1st English Edition 2017

Boca Raton, FL USA
2020

SUMMARY

Preface	9
CHAPTER ONE — Who we are, and why are we here?	11
CHAPTER TWO — What happened to us?	21
CHAPTER THREE — Who Can Save Us?	29
CHAPTER FOUR — How Can I Change?	39
CHAPTER FIVE — Which path should i take now?	51

PREFACE

*F*or centuries, philosophers and scholars around the world have tried their best to understand the purpose of human life, and answer the age-old question, "Why are we here?"

Humanity is currently experiencing one of the biggest existential crisis in history. While acknowledging our place as unique, intelligent, and gifted beings, capable of making great discoveries and overcoming extreme obstacles, mankind has long taken a turn for the worse. We are left baffled by the fact man has become so selfish, proud, ungrateful, disrespectful, cruel, corrupt, greedy, arrogant, and evil. At times, we even fail to understand our own actions and behavior. We want to change the world, but we cannot even change ourselves! What can we do?

The author, Dong Yu Lan, talks about the true purpose of man's creation and the events that shaped mankind since. He also expounds on God's work to rescue man from misery and give him a new life. This book will help you understand God's expectations for man, and what He has prepared for us in the coming age.

The author hopes that this book will inspire you to have a new life; one that is full of joy and inner quality. Once you have found the help you need, we hope that you will share these encouraging words, so the people around you can understand the true meaning of human life.

São Paulo, September 2010.

The Editors

CHAPTER ONE

WHO WE ARE, AND WHY ARE WE HERE?

The Meaning of Human Life

What is the meaning of human life? What is the true purpose of our lives? Are we merely here to eat, work, accomplish something, have fun, study, have a family, sleep, and ultimately die?

No living being has ever been able to surpass man; we are undoubtedly wonderful creatures. While physically weaker than some animals, our consciousness makes up for our frailty in the form of feelings and ability to reason.

In addition to being the highest created life, human life is unrivaled and unique. Why do we have such an elevated life? For centuries, philosophers and scholars from around the world have attempted to decipher the meaning of human life, yet never taking its origin and Creator into consideration.

To find out the purpose of a certain product, you need to go to the source, the manufacturer. Likewise, if we want to know why we were created, we must go to God, our Creator.

The Bible, which is the Word of God, tells us that God created man as a vessel (Genesis 2:7; Isaiah 45:9; 2 Corinthians. 4:7). It is obvious that the purpose of a vessel is to contain something. Therefore, as vessels, what were we created to contain? What can truly fill and satisfy us? Is it knowledge, accomplishments, fame, travels, culture, or money? While these things can provide a temporary sense of pleasure, they cannot take away the feeling that something is missing. The Bible talks about that in Isaiah 55:2: "Why do you spend money for what is not bread, and your wages for what does not satisfy?"

Have you ever felt hungry and thirsty within? We try to satisfy this inner hunger by buying something at the mall, by going to a restaurant, or by watching sports with our friends; still, the emptiness remains. We try many things, but nothing can truly quench our inner thirst. Do you know why? It is because what we long for cannot be found in those places.

The creation of man has a much higher purpose than we are led to believe. We have a mind to think, emotions to feel, and a will to decide what we want. Together, these three parts make up the human soul. However, only a few people know that man has something other than his soul, something deeper, called the human spirit. Now the spirit of man is what compels us to seek something higher, better, and more important, which is God himself. We must not ignore or reject this yearning: "They always go astray in their heart, and they have not known My ways" (Hebrews 3:10b); "The wicked are estranged from the womb; they go astray as soon as they are born, speaking lies" (Psalms 58:3).

The Creation of Man: In the Image and Likeness of The Creator

Unlike the rest of creation, man was created in a very special way. God created us as vessels to contain Himself as life. (Romans 9:23-24; 2 Corinthians 4:7). The first book of the Bible, Genesis, tells us that God said, "Let Us make man in Our image, according to Our likeness" (1:26).

All the living things God created before man were created "according to their kind" (Genesis 1:11, 12, 21, 24-25). Man, however, was created after God's own image and likeness (vv. 26-27). Just like a glove bears the likeness of a hand, which it was made to contain, man was created to receive God as his content, that he might express Him. Our mind, emotion, and will were created after God's image, which is Christ himself (2 Corinthians 4:4). Without God, however, these inherent faculties and abilities are limited and purposeless, as they were created to receive and function with the divine element of God's life.

The Three Parts of Man

Now, let us see how God created man: "And the LORD God formed man of the dust of the ground, and breathed into his nostrils the breath of life; and man became a living being" (Genesis 2:7). God used the dust of the ground as "raw material" to make the human body, and breathed the breath of life into his nostrils, which became the spirit of man. The Hebrew word for "breath of life," neshamah, is also found in Proverbs 20:27, referring to "the spirit" of man. In other words, God's breath of life became the spirit of man. After receiving the breath of life, that lifeless clay shell became a living soul (see the diagram).

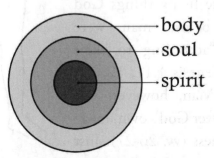

The human body possesses the bios life, a biological life composed of water, nitrogen, carbon, iron, and other chemical elements found in the ground; hence, "from the dust of the ground." Although man has managed to prolong his biological life through science, his body is mortal and limited by space and time.

In addition to his body, man has a hidden, mysterious, and deeper inner part – his soul, which is his psyche, the psychological part of his being.

Within our soul, we have a mind to think (Psalms 139:14; Lamentations 3:20); emotions to feel love, hatred, joy, sadness, etc (1 Samuel 18:1; Psalm 42:1; Isaiah 61:10); and a will to make decisions (Job 7:15; Daniel 1:8). In other words, our being is made of more than just the dust of the ground, which is why we can live, think, feel, and decide.

God has a plan, a good pleasure, and a will, which is His mystery. Our soul was made in God's image, and all its three parts match Him: man was given a mind to understand God's plan; emotions to feel God's good pleasure, that is, to love what He loves and hate what He hates; and a will to receive and accept the divine will.

Now deep within man lies a part that is hidden, mysterious, and even deeper than his soul – the spirit of man. As marrow is hidden within the bones, so is the spirit of man in his soul. The spirit and soul of man are so close together that they are often confused with one another. Nevertheless, 1 Thessalonians 5:23 speaks of the tree parts of man clearly and distinctly: "Now may the God of peace Himself sanctify you completely; and may your whole spirit [pneuma], soul [psyche], and body [soma] be preserved blameless at the coming of our Lord Jesus Christ." Hebrews 4:12 also makes a distinction between spirit and soul, indicating that the Word of God is sharp enough to separate the two.

The spirit of man longs for that which is divine and eternal (Ecclesiastes 3:11). God created man for Himself, so only God can fulfill him. Without God as its content, the spirit of man is forever restless, empty, and perpetually searching for something real. While the mind can think, only the spirit of man can contact God, for God is Spirit (John 4:24). The spirit of man is his most important part before God. Zechariah 12:1 reads, "The LORD, who stretches out the heavens, lays the foundation of the earth, and forms the spirit of man within him." Based on the Word of God, the importance of the spirit of man is matched only by the creation of the heavens and earth. Moreover, the Lord Jesus said that the Father seeks true worshipers, who worship in spirit and truth (John 4:23).

The spirit of man is also composed of three parts: intuition (Mark 2:8; 1 Corinthians 2:11), fellowship (John 4:24; 1 Corinthians 6:17; Ephesians 6:18), and conscience (Romans 8:16; 9:1). When God desires to speak to us, He does it directly through our intuition, that we may discern His will. The fellowship in our spirit provides a two-way communication line between God and us.

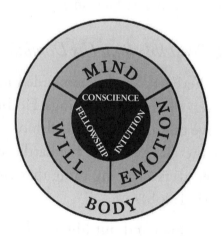

Finally, God created our conscience as a link between our spirit and soul. Our conscience is meant to help all three parts of our soul submit to and heed the will of God (Hebrews 9:14b). The three parts of our soul, along with our conscience, make up the heart of man. The conscience leads and compels the heart of man to turn to God, to love Him, and to follow Him (Matthew 22:37).

God's Purpose in Creating Man

A. Having A Helper as His Counterpart

As previously mentioned, God has a plan (a purpose), which is His good pleasure (satisfaction) and will (Ephesians 1:9). Now in order to fulfill His good pleasure, God created man as His counterpart. After He created man, God said, "It is not good that man should be alone; I will make him a helper comparable to him" (Genesis 2:18). Likewise, God created us to be His counterpart, His satisfaction.

B. Reestablishing His Dominion

Over All the Earth God commanded man to have dominion over all the living things He had created: "Let them have dominion over the fish of the sea, over the birds of the air, and over the cattle, over all the earth and over every creeping thing that creeps on the earth" (Genesis 1:26b).

God created man and put him on the earth, where His divine government had been usurped by Satan, His enemy. He wanted to reclaim the earth for Himself by means of the man He created. In other words, God created man to usher in His authority, subdue His enemy, and restore His kingdom on earth (v. 28).

God created man with a free will, but His desire was that man would choose Him and receive Him as life. His desire was to enter the spirit of man, dwell there, and then spread into the soul of man, that He might express His authority and reclaim His dominion over the earth.

Now that we know these amazing spiritual facts, let us worship the Lord and pray, *"Oh Lord, You are my God! Thank You for creating me in such a special way! I confess I did not know Your plan for me. Come into me and fill me with Your life! Without You, I am always empty and dissatisfied. I need You, Lord! I give myself to You and I want to be useful in Your hands, that You be satisfied and Your will be done in me. Amen!"*

Chapter Two

WHAT HAPPENED TO US?

The Ruin of Human Life

In the previous chapter, we learned that we were created in a unique way, after the Creator's image and likeness. God made us for a noble cause: to receive Him as life, that we may usher in His expression, authority, dominion, and kingdom on earth to defeat His enemy.

Why, then, can we not live up to such a noble purpose? Why do we not have the quality of life we desire? What happened to us?

You just have to look around to see the inner conflict and endless pursuit for satisfaction distressing people all around the world. Some people are rich, famous, intelligent, and yet live a miserable life. Others, rather than pursuing the holiness of God, have chosen to express immoral and sordid human traits, spreading evil, malice, corruption, and violence wherever they go. Corrupted and ruined by sin, man has become a dirty vessel in the "sewer" of society.

Sin Entered Man

After creating man, God put him in the garden of Eden. His desire was that he would eat of the tree of life, in the middle of the garden, which represented God himself as life. If man had eaten of that tree, he would have lived forever. God specifically warned him not to eat of the tree of knowledge of good and evil, or else he would surely die (Genesis 2:17). So why did Adam and Eve eat it?

The Cunning Serpent

Aware of God's plan, Satan waited around until man was vulnerable. Then, before man ate of the tree of life, Satan, also described as the old serpent in the Bible due to his cunningness (Revelation 12:9; 20:2), deceived the woman: "Now the serpent was more cunning than any beast of the field which the LORD God had made. And he said to the woman, 'Has God indeed said, 'You shall not eat of every tree of the garden?' (Genesis 3:1).

Satan's first strategy was to make the woman doubt God's Word. This is one of his oldest tricks. Have this ever happened to you? Have you ever doubted God's Word? Has anyone ever said something to you or sent you a message on the internet that made you doubt what the Bible says? The woman ended up falling into Satan's trap (vv. 2-3). Despite her attempt to defend what God had said, she became vulnerable to Satan's craftiness the moment she opened up to argue with him. After sowing the seed of doubt, Satan openly and bluntly rebutted God's command to man. Although God had already warned man, saying, "for in the day that you eat of it you shall surely die" (Genesis 2:17b), Satan contradict God's word and added something, "You will not surely die. For God knows that in the day you eat of it your eyes will be opened, and you will be like God, knowing good and evil" (3:4-5).

Satan had managed to instigate man and woman to become independent from God. That was the beginning of humanity's downfall. Satan neither slandered God directly, nor tried to turn the woman against Him right away. Instead, he subtly persuaded Eve to act on her own, without consulting God, her husband, or her spirit. While the serpent's questions led her to doubt God, his suggestions incited her to desire the fruit God had commanded them not to eat.

Once seduced by Satan's arguments and seeing that the tree was good for food, pleasant to the eyes, and desirable to make one wise, Eve took its fruit and ate it, and gave it to her husband, and he ate it (Genesis 3:1-6). This seemingly small act brought about chaos to all creation. When sin entered humanity, it brought along the sinful nature, yielding death and rebellion.

This evil nature made man inherently sinful, meaning that all men became subject to and overcome by the element of death. Death is the consequence of sin, "For the wages of sin is death" (Romans 6:23a). Not only was man affected by sin, but the whole creation was subject to futility and corruption (8:20-22).

The Consequence of Sin

Let us use the innocence of a child to illustrate the disobedience of Adam and Eve. Suppose the parents of a young boy warn him to stay away from certain bottles on the shelf containing toxic substance. Then, one day, someone approaches that boy, makes him doubt what his parents told him, and he ends up drinking what was in those bottles.

Although picking up those bottles was already a transgression of his parents' loving warning, drinking their content was much worse. It may take a while, but that toxic substance will surely harm and corrupt the boy from within. Should his condition go untreated, it may even lead to death.

When man ate of the tree of knowledge of good and evil, not only did he transgress God's Word, but he was also contaminated by a sinful, corrupt, and evil nature. After entering man, this sinful nature, which the Bible calls "sin," damaged and altered his behavior, deeds, thoughts, and words. Man's body became a body of sin and death, in which no good abides (7:20-24).

This evil nature also affected man's relationship with the Creator (Luke 3:7; John 8:44). After being deceived by Satan, man fled God's presence and distanced himself from Him, so his impurities would not be exposed. When man failed to exercise his spirit, which allows him to enjoy fellowship with God, he ended up choosing to eat of the tree of knowledge of good and evil. To this day, whenever man fails to use his spirit, he becomes an easy target for the snares of the devil.

As for the soul, which is the human psyche created to follow the spirit's leading, it became independent, autonomous. No longer seeking the conscience for guidance, the soul felt able to discern good from evil without God. The soul of man developed a life of its own; a life riddled with its own opinions and a false sense that it does not need God to discern right from wrong. We call this independent and autonomous life "the soul-life."

Instead of leading Adam and Eve back to the only One who could help them, God, this supposed discerning ability made them fear Him and hide after realizing their nakedness. What a big mistake!

The human soul became evil and filled with things that oppose God. The mind became darkened and unable to understand the things of God, aimlessly wandering through the futility of its own thoughts (Ephesians 4:17-18). The emotion, which was created to love God, started loving many other things (2 Timothy 3:2-4). Finally, the will of man, created to choose and obey God, became obstinate for its own things, and rebelled against the Lord (Ephesians 4:19).

When the first man, Adam, ate of the tree of knowledge of good and evil, he missed the opportunity of allowing God's life to enter his being. An entire race emerged from him, and we are a part of it (1 Corinthians 15:45-49). We all inherited Adam's corruption and fallen nature – the lusts of the flesh, an independent soul, a deadened spirit, and death (Romans 5:12).

Our whole being – spirit, soul, and body – was affected and damaged when the evil nature came in. Man, who was created to express God and restore His authority on earth, became one with the current of this world, subject to the evil powers working in the sons of disobedience and the desires of the flesh and mind (Ephesians 2:2-3). Many people, who are inwardly dead, choose to utterly disregard the existence of God. Having no fear of God, they live a dissolute life, deceiving and being deceived by their own greed.

The fact sin is inside of us means that we have all sinned (Romans 3:23; 5:12). We all have a nature that is contrary to God, an inherent element that binds us to sin and separates us from God. This is something that can be observed in our daily living. Although we may not want to, we end up lying, getting angry, becoming conceited, and even giving place to hatred. Others even commit blunter sins such as stealing, adultery, murder, etc. Man cannot escape his evil nature – he wants to do good, but ends up doing the evil he does not want to (7:18, 20).

Because of our sinful nature, God's divine judgment, resulting condemnation, and wrath are upon us all (5:18; John 3:36). He will exact His judgement on all those who remain in this condition. They will be cast into the lake of fire, which was not made for man, but for Satan and the angels who followed him in his rebellion against God (Matthew 25:41; Revelation 20:15). Having become a slave to Satan, following him and doing his bidding, man is doomed to share his fate; that is, death, followed by the lake of fire. What a dreadful, wretched situation! Who can deliver us from this fate?

Humanity is hopeless to rescue itself from such degraded, deplorable condition. In the next chapter, we will see that God devised a most wonderful plan to save man. Despite the distance, God never gave up on the man He created. The path He took to save us, that we may have a life with purpose and inner quality, exhibits His great love and wisdom.

Chapter Three

WHO CAN SAVE US?

Rescuing Human Life

The book of Ephesians describes man's deplorable situation after sin entered him: "And you He made alive, who were dead in trespasses and sins, in which you once walked according to the course of this world, according to the prince of the power of the air, the spirit who now works in the sons of disobedience, among whom also we all once conducted ourselves in the lusts of our flesh, fulfilling the desires of the flesh and of the mind, and were by nature children of wrath, just as the others" (2:1-3).

The fall diverted humanity from God's original intent, ruining and corrupting it with the evil nature. Man's deeds and transgressions made him all the more reprehensible before God's righteous judgment. God, however, relinquished neither the man He created, nor

His desire to use him to restore His authority on earth. For that reason, God himself came down to carry out His redeeming work.

The Motivation to Rescue the Lost Ones

The driving force behind God's redeeming work, which gave our lives purpose and inner quality, is His love: "But God, who is rich in mercy, because of His great love with which He loved us, even when we were dead in trespasses, made us alive together with Christ [by grace you have been saved]" (Ephesians 2:4-5). Unworthy of His love, God would have been right to abandon us. Still, moved by His great love and mercy, He saved us from misery and brought us to a place where we can enjoy His presence and love.

God's great love and mercy are copiously exhibited in the three parables of Luke 15. We were weary, scattered, and shepherdless when the Good Shepherd left His glory to find us, His lost sheep (vv. 3-7). Despite our little worth, like that of a lost silver coin, God searched for us diligently until He found us (vv. 8-10).

We were rebellious, independent, and frustrated within, living a life on our own terms to fulfil our dreams. Still, at the slightest sign of repentance, that is, when we take but one step towards Him, God takes all the necessary measures to bring us back to Him (vv. 11-32). What a great love!

A Great Requirement, A High Price, and A Noble Sacrifice

The New Testament shows us that, in order to bring man back to Himself, God carried out a work of redemption; that is, a work to recover something that had been lost.

Since God is the origin and Creator of all things, including us, we belong to Him. However, because of the deceit of sin, we became lost in this world as the sheep, the silver coin, and the prodigal son mentioned in Luke 15. Who would pay the price to save us? Only someone who loves us very much, God.

In order to fulfill God's three requirements to redeem us – righteousness, holiness, and glory –, the Lord paid an exceedingly high price. As corrupt and filthy men, we could not pay it ourselves. Having fallen into the "great sewer of sin," humanity was powerless to help itself. Then, God did something divine, mysterious, and wonderful, that He might rescue man from that great filth, cleanse him, purify him, and take him back. Human words simply fail to express the greatness of God's redeeming work, sending His own Son into that "sewer of sin," which is the world, to save us (John 3:16-17). Having lived here for thirty-three and a half years, the Son of God died on the cross to redeem us. Only a great love could have done that!

God himself came down to fulfill His righteous

requirements by paying a high price to redeem us. His noble sacrifice involved the death of His Son, His only begotten Son, Jesus Christ: "For when we were still without strength, in due time Christ died for the ungodly. For scarcely for a righteous man will one die; yet perhaps for a good man someone would even dare to die. But God demonstrates His own love toward us, in that while we were still sinners, Christ died for us" (Romans 5:6-8). In other words, Christ died for our sins once and for all, the Righteous for the unrighteous, that He might bring us back to God (1 Peter 3:18).

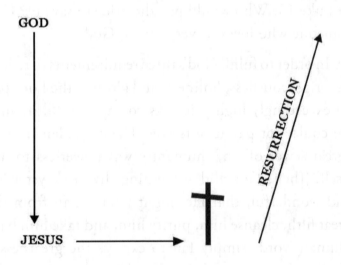

Being neither righteous nor holy, there was no way for us to pay that price. We were lost, enemies of God, expressing only the result of the fall. Since the wages of sin is death, our fate was to perish in our sins (Romans 6:23). Thanks to the Lord, however, Christ died in our place and carried out redemption; that is, He paid a high price to redeem us to God and for His purpose. The high price He paid was one of blood: "knowing that you were not redeemed with corruptible things, like silver or gold, from your aimless conduct (...) but with the precious blood of Christ, as of a lamb without blemish and without spot" (1 Peter 1:18-19).

Through the death of Jesus, man, who is unrighteous, can be justified before God and return to Him. Sinners can find forgiveness, change their position, and receive God's life. By the blood of Jesus, even a man who was an enemy of God can be reconciled to Him, entering His presence boldly (2 Corinthians 5:19; Hebrews 10:19-22). After Jesus, the Son of God, was delivered to death for our trespasses, God approved His work and raised Him for our justification. What a wonderful redemption!

Regaining a Life with Inner Quality

Knowing the redemption of Christ and believing in what He has done for us is essential to having a life with inner quality. Unless you know in your conscience that your sins were forgiven, you simply cannot enjoy such inner quality. Have you ever offended a friend? If so, you felt bad about it, right? Well, knowing that we have sinned against God should make us feel much more uncomfortable. Many people carry a feeling of accusation and the fear of eternal condemnation their whole lives. Through the redemption of Christ, however, everyone who believes in Him has the forgiveness of sins (Acts 10:43). This means that, before God, the record of our sins has been removed. In other words, by believing in Christ, we are freed from God's righteous judgment; that is, we will be judged for the sins committed in the past (John 3:18).

When the Son of God died and shed His blood for us, forgiving us and removing our transgressions, all of God's righteous requirements were fulfilled (Psalms 103:12). God also wiped out the handwriting of requirements that was against us, having nailed it to the cross by means of Christ's death (Colossians 2:14-15). When we believe in God, His rich mercy causes Him to remember our sins no more (Hebrews 8:12), and His righteousness moves Him to forgive us of our sins and cleanse us from all unrighteousness. What a great relief it is to know that our past sins were canceled out and our unrighteousness cleansed away! What a blessing it is to have a conscience free of offenses! What freedom!

Man's Cooperation in Being Delivered Inwardly

Up to this point in our reading, we have touched upon everything God has done to redeem us to Himself. Now, we will get into the steps needed to enjoy the forgiveness of sins, the wiping out of the record against us, our justification, our sanctification, and our reconciliation with God.

The first step is to be enlightened by God's Word. Only through His Word can we see our true condition, who we truly are. In addition to exposing our outward mistakes, our shortcomings, God's Word illuminates the depths of our being, manifesting the intentions and purposes of our heart (Matthew 4:16; John 8:7-9; Hebrews 4:12-13).

Once we are enlightened, we must immediately repent; that is, we must have a change of mind. When we were in darkness, we could not see that our path was contrary to God. Then, the moment we heard the Lord's Word, our hearts were constrained by it; we felt repentant within and eager to turn to God, walk on His path, and do His will (Luke 24:32; Acts 2:37).

The next step is to believe in God's Word and in the name of Jesus. When we believe in Christ, we enter into Him and are joined to Him. Since believing is receiving, believing in Christ means receiving everything He has done for us. By believing in Christ, who is righteous and holy, we too can be righteous and holy, which means to be set apart for God. Finally, by believing that Christ died for us, that we might be reconciled to God, we can have peace towards God! What a holy change! We must never forget that these things are only possible because of God's great love toward us.

While enjoying this organic oneness with Christ, we spontaneously confess our sins and transgressions, as they are revealed by God's Word. When we confess our sins and lay hold of the blood of Jesus, our conscience is cleansed from dead works (Hebrews 9:14). Moreover, as we confess our sins, the blood of Christ speaks and intercedes on our behalf against the accuser, Satan, who accuses us before God (Revelation 12:10). This way, our repentance becomes known to God's enemy, Satan. The more thorough our confession is, the stronger our ground to overcome the accuser (v. 11).

As a result of being forgiven by God, we are delivered from all our inner fears, that we may learn to fear and consider God in all our ways and deeds: "But there is forgiveness with You, that You may be feared" (Psalms 130:4). God's forgiveness also begets in us a strong love for Him. Though we were worthy of condemnation, He forgave us; that is why we love Him (Luke 7:47).

We thank God for His plan to redeem us to Himself. We can only bless and worship Him:

"Oh Lord, my God, I am so grateful that You sent Your Son to die for me. Your great love moved You to go into the "trash can of sin" where I was to save me.

Lord Jesus, thank You for Your precious blood! You paid my debt on the cross and bought me back to God. Lord, I repent from living a life alienated from You, offending both You and my neighbor. Thank You for forgiving me and for wiping out the record of my sins before God. Thank You for giving me a new life, so that I may fear and love You all my days. Amen."

CHAPTER FOUR

HOW CAN I CHANGE?

A New Life for a New Beginning

In the previous chapter, we learned that Christ died and shed His blood to deal with our sins before God. We were forgiven from our sins, and their record was wiped out. His redeeming work delivered us from a past of transgressions against God. We were justified, sanctified, and reconciled to God by believing in Christ and the work He carried out on the cross. His redemption cleansed our conscience of dead works and provided us a solid foundation against Satan's accusations. What a great blessing!

In order to have a life with purpose and inner quality we need something more. In addition to forgiving o past sins and cleansing us by means of His own blc God wants to give us a new life and free us from old nature. His desire is to cleanse us from all filth and make us a new creation (Ephesians 2:1, 5; Galatians 5:19-22, 24; 6:15; 2 Corinthians 5:17). God wants to fill us with Himself, supplying us with life, joy, strength, and inner peace.

Without the divine life, human life is fleeting at best (1 Peter 1:24). It has a beginning and an end; an entrance and an exit. We all come from dust and return to dust (Ecclesiastes 3:20). Human life is indeed short and, without understanding its true meaning and purpose, people try to "make the most of their days," constantly seeking to appease their fleshly desires. Others even try to "bride" their own conscience by doing good deeds. They spend their lives running after things that are worthless, and, whether or not they get what they want, they still feel empty, dry, restless, and frustrated in the end.

We all have our trials and, sometimes, it seems we are sailing against the current and the wind. The worst part is realizing that, in addition to the obstacles we must overcome in our journey, there is a "hole in our boat." It is quite hard to acknowledge that our biggest frustration lies in trying to change who we are. When we see holes in our boat, we often consider, "If I go on this way, will I make it to the end? It would be really nice if I could change."

Attempting to ignore the "hole in their boat," people struggle to overcome their limitations and achieve their goals as fast as they can. After all, time does not wait for anyone. However, the so-called "winners" still get frustrated, often thinking to themselves, "Was it all worth it?"

King Solomon, one of the wisest kings who ever lived, described this feeling quite well: "I made my works great, I built myself houses, and planted myself vineyards. I made myself gardens and orchards, and I planted all kinds of fruit trees in them. I made myself water pools from which to water the growing trees of the grove. I acquired male and female servants, and had servants born in my house. Yes, I had greater possessions of herds and flocks than all who were in Jerusalem before me. I also gathered for myself silver and gold and the special treasures of kings and of the provinces. I acquired male and female singers, the delights of the sons of men, and musical instruments of all kinds. So I became great and excelled more than all who were before me in Jerusalem. Also my wisdom remained with me. Whatever my eyes desired I did not keep from them. I did not withhold my heart from any pleasure, for my heart rejoiced in all my labor; and this was my reward from all my labor. Then I looked on all the works that my hands had done and on the labor in which I had toiled; and indeed all was vanity and grasping for the wind. There was no profit under the sun" (Ecclesiastes 12: 4-11).

King Solomon's experience makes it clear that, though we strive to overcome adversity, fulfill our dreams, and achieve our goals, everything is fleeting and vain. We run back and forth, work hard, and everything still vanishes in the end in an instant. Then, we start all over again – we set new objectives, work towards achieving them, and eventually find ourselves back at square one. It is like running after the wind. We may be rich in money and achievements, and still feel dry and empty inside. The older we get, the more we become aware of our "boat's" impending fate: that it will sink sooner or later. What can we do?

Amid this inner crisis, we realize that we need to change, not just on the outside, but inwardly. We need a new "boat;" that is, a new life. We need to be born again, be regenerated, that we may receive a life that is divine and eternal. If we truly want to have a fresh start, we must be born of God!

The Importance of Being Born Again

The Bible tells us that the Lord Jesus said to Nicodemus, "You must be born again" (John 3:7). Despite his high position as a Pharisee, a teacher of Jewish religion, and a chief Jew, Nicodemus felt troubled inside, which led him to seek Jesus. He was probably dissatisfied with the life he had, and felt a sense of purposelessness. After realizing that there was something special about Jesus, who inspired others to live by a different principle of life, Nicodemus went looking for Him at night.

As a ruler of the Jews, one with a high status and social recognition, Nicodemus was expected to be a pattern for the people in fulfilling his duties. Moreover, being an expert in the Jewish religion, a Pharisee, and a keeper of God's law, Nicodemus was certainly a moral man. He was a respected elder with substantial human experience – he knew what to do, how to behave, how to talk to people, and also practiced good deeds. We can tell that he was a humble man because, despite being older than Jesus, he addressed Him as Rabbi, which means Teacher. Being someone highly educated, a teacher in Israel, Nicodemus taught others to do good and live according to the law.

It is quite remarkable that someone with a "resume" like that of Nicodemus – with such admirable virtues, refined character, and career – would lack something.

Despite all that he was and had, Nicodemus' attitude exposed his lack of inner quality of life. He may have believed that being a good, religious, learned, and socially high-ranked person was the purpose of his life. Those things, however, could not provide him the quality of life for which he had been looking. Perhaps he had been feeling that his "boat" was sinking. When he came to Jesus, Nicodemus could not hide his admiration for His deeds, which, according to him, no man could do unless God was with him (John 3: 2). The questions he asked the Lord conveyed his unrest as to how he could change his life.

The Lord Jesus simply told Nicodemus that, "unless one is born again, he cannot see the kingdom of God." Despite his expertise in religion, he knew nothing about being born again. Although he understood human life and the culture of the nation of Israel, he did not know how to enter the kingdom of God in its spiritual aspect. He had no knowledge on regeneration; that is, on being born again. His high position, power, knowledge, and influence could not help him enter the spiritual, divine, eternal, and heavenly kingdom. He had to be born again.

Two Steps to Enter into Man and Give Him Life

According to the Bible, God created man after His own image and likeness to receive His divine, eternal life. Genesis 2:7-9 tells us that, after being created, man was placed in front of the tree of life, which represents God himself. His desire was that man would choose Him and receive Him as life. If man had eaten of this tree, he would have matured in the divine life and attained God's expression, restoring His authority and kingdom on earth.

However, having chosen to eat of the tree of knowledge of good and evil, death entered man and spread to all mankind. Still, as His purpose is immutable, God took two steps to deal with men's problem:

First, God became a man, Jesus: "And the Word [God] became flesh and dwelt among us" (John 1:14). As the Son of Man, He came in the likeness of sinful flesh, so that God would condemn sin in His flesh, and destroy him who has the power of death, the devil (Romans 8:3; Hebrews 2:14-15). After He died, God took the second step – He raised Jesus on the third day, and declared Him to be the Son of God with power. Christ became the life-giving Spirit, that He might enter the spirit of those who believe in Him and give them eternal life, God's life (Romans 1:4; 1 Corinthians 15:45b; John 7:39).

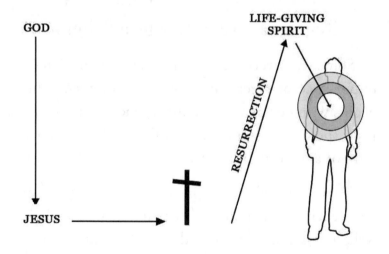

By means of His death and resurrection, Jesus fulfilled what He had told His disciples: "Most assuredly, I say to you, unless a grain of wheat falls into the ground and dies, it remains alone; but if it dies, it produces much grain" (John 12:24). After the "grain of wheat" fell into the ground and died, it reemerged to produce many "grains;" that is, many children to God.

All who believe in Jesus have the divine life, are born of the Spirit, and have been regenerated unto a living hope (John 3:5; 1 Peter 1:3). Since he who has the Son has life (1 John 5:12), those who have the divine life have the hope of transformation. They have a life with inner quality, knowing that they will be changed within and made useful for God's purpose.

The Difference Between Being Regenerated and Having a Religion

Some believers fail to properly appreciate the importance of regeneration. God's entire work in us begins with our new birth, our regeneration. The Lord Jesus spoke of this matter with the disciples, who also did not appreciate it at first.

Having failed to appreciate this matter, some people have turned their Christian lives into a religion. Religion is nothing more than an attempt to please God by our own human effort; it is striving to live a life according to the traditions of our forefathers, which often annul and oppose God's Word (Mark 7:8, 13; 1 Peter 1:18). It also induces people to try to fix their "old boats," their old lives, on their own, without God. Such people do not know God inwardly; they have never truly prayed to receive Him. Despite knowing their laws and traditions, they are far away from God's will. At the time of Jesus, for instance, the religious people despised and even wanted to kill Him. They were always ready and willing to condemn those who transgressed their laws and traditions (John 8:3-6; 9:16, 28-34).

In the previous chapter, we learned that, in addition to being unclean, we were dead in our sins. Only God's life could change our inward condition. It is one thing to put makeup on a corpse, and a whole other thing to give it life. While religion is concerned with the outward appearance, "putting makeup on the corpse," God wants us to know Him by receiving Jesus, whom He sent to save us from eternal condemnation, that we may have a new, eternal life (John 17:3).

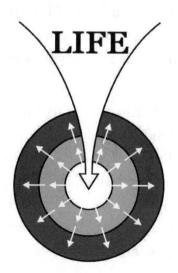

When we believe in the Son of God, He comes into us and enlivens our spirit. Having begun in our spirit, God's ultimate desire is to enliven our whole being.

In addition to a Creator-creation relationship, God desires to have a Father-son relationship with man. Hence, the Bible tells us that all who believe in the name of Jesus are given the power to become God's children (John 1:12). Being born of God is the greatest miracle man can experience. When we were born again, we, who are creatures, received the Creator's life. This is wonderful!

The Characteristics of This New Life

Being regenerated means that an incorruptible seed was sown into us by the gospel; that is, by God's Word (1 Peter 1:23, 25). As a seed, it spontaneously grows, matures, blossoms, and bears fruit. You do not have to tell an orange tree to bear oranges; you just provide what it needs to grow, and it will bear oranges in due time.

Our new birth also ushers us into a realm of life, the realm of God's kingdom. Those who are born anew have a life from above, a heavenly life (John 3:3, 31). Just as our human parents ushered us into the human kingdom, we were ushered into God's kingdom when we believed in Jesus and were born of God. Before regeneration, we were exclusively earthly and our minds were constantly set on the things of the earth. After receiving the divine life, however, we began thinking and seeking the things from above, the things pertaining to God's kingdom (Colossians 3:1-2; Matthew 6:33).

Having been regenerated, we now have two lives within us – one out of the flesh, and the other out of the Spirit. We inherited our fleshly life from Adam. As for our new life, which we received from the Spirit, we inherited it from God. Having been born of the flesh, we are flesh, which is why we are prone to sin. Our fallen human nature, which is unable to submit to the law of God, compels us to sin (Romans 8:7-8). The old life we inherited from our parents has sold itself out to sin; it is completely alienated from God's life and unable to understand the things of God (1 Corinthians 2:14). In addition to making us children of God, this new life we received through regeneration teaches us all that is true and leads us to know our Father.

This new life in our spirit is divine, and so it rejects sin (1 John 5:18). For instance, one of the main differences between a duck and a chicken is that ducks like to go in the water, but chickens do not. They behave differently because they are inherently different. By nature, ducks are fond of water, just as the life we inherited from Adam is fond of sin. On the other hand, chickens do not enjoy water, just as the divine life within us rejects sin. These inherent characteristics do not need to be taught.

If we choose to live by the divine life within us, which is in our spirit, we will spontaneously bear the fruit of this life: love, joy, peace, longsuffering, kindness, goodness, faithfulness, gentleness, and self-control (Galatians 5:22-23). On the other hand, if we continue living by the old life, we will produce the works of death: hatred, contentions, jealousies, outbursts of wrath, selfish ambitions, dissensions, etc. (Galatians 5:19-21).

Another important characteristic of the divine life, which we received through regeneration, is the ability to love God and those begotten of Him, our brethren in Christ. God is love and, as children of love, we spontaneously love our brethren (1 John 3:14; 4:21). What is more, the love out of this new life is unconditional! God does not require us to love Him first, that He may love us in return. In other words, the love out of the divine life does not require reciprocity. While human love is selfish, the divine love gives and sacrifices itself for the sake of others.

The moment we believed in the Lord Jesus and called on His name, "Oh Lord Jesus," we received a new life, God's life. What a glorious new beginning! Still, God desires this new life within us to grow and transform us, until we are like Him in life and nature (1 John 3: 2). The more His divine life grows in us, the closer we get to fulfilling His purpose for our lives – having a life with purpose and inner quality.

Chapter Five

WHICH PATH SHOULD I TAKE NOW?

Practical Lessons for A Life with Purpose and Inner Quality

*A*s mentioned in previous chapters, the Bible left us a solid foundation concerning how and why God created man. We also learned that, the moment man was deceived and enslaved by sin, a great tragedy befell the entire universe. Amid this seemingly hopeless situation, God, moved by His great love, sent His Son to die in our place and bring us back to Himself. What is more, He gave us a new beginning by giving us His life and making us His sons through regeneration. That was a true miracle! We no longer need to live as slaves to sin! Now that we have a new life, we can be delivered from this world's angst and anxiety. When we first believed in the Lord Jesus with our hearts, and called on His name with our mouths, "Oh Lord Jesus," we received the eternal life and were saved in our spirit.

Regeneration is a milestone in the lives of all who believe in the Lord Jesus. God Himself dwells in us today; we are one Spirit with Him (1 Corinthians 6:17). Having received the eternal life, the salvation of our spirit is also eternal (John 3:16). The Bible assures our salvation, saying, "He who has the Son has life" (1 John 5:12). When we believed in the Son of God, we received His divine, eternal life, which means we will never perish (John 10:28).

We must not stop at this stage of our journey with Christ, as God's purpose for us goes far beyond regeneration. As mentioned in the first chapter of this book, man is a tripartite being composed of spirit, soul, and body, all of which were affected by the evil nature of sin. We need the divine life to have a life with inner quality (Romans 5:10b). God wants His divine life to reach every part of our being, sanctifying, saving, and keeping us whole unto Him (Philippians 2:12, 1 Thessalonians 5:23). In other words, beginning from within us, from our spirit, God wants to enliven our whole being with His life.

Calling on The Name of The Lord

Our new birth enlivened our spirit (Romans 8:10b) and made us children of God. Now, His desire is that His children may grow and mature. A child needs to breathe normally, eat well, drink plenty of water every day, exercise, and rest to grow and develop in a healthy way.

This can also be applied spiritually. We need to go before the Lord every morning in prayer, that we may be renewed and enlivened. The moment we wake up, we must set aside some time to have fellowship with the Lord.

In order to turn our whole being to Him, we can call on His name from deep within, "Oh Lord Jesus! Oh Lord Jesus!" As we call on His name, we "breathe out" everything that is spiritually choking us – our fears, sadness, sins, etc – and "breathe in" the Lord Jesus as life, joy, peace, strength, and encouragement. If you call on the name of the Lord Jesus several times during your day, you will surely remain in His presence and light. What is more, you will experience His continuous salvation and enjoy all His riches (Romans 10:12-13).

Pray-Reading and Practicing the Lord's Word

The new life we received from Christ also needs to be daily supplied with God's Word. We must long for God's Word as a newborn baby longs for its mother's milk, that we may grow unto salvation (1 Peter 2:1-2). The Word of God nourishes our faith, that we may grow into godliness; that is, into being like God. Preferably during the first hours of your day, learn to turn some Bible verses into prayer, slowly repeating and proclaiming them, as if you were chewing on food to extract all its nutrients. Instead of worrying about understanding the verse, just eat it: "Your words were found, and I ate them, and Your word was to me the joy and rejoicing of my heart; for I am called by Your name, O LORD God of hosts" (Jeremiah 15:16). When you turn the Word into your prayer, you fellowship with the Lord and live by Him (John 6:57).[1]

In addition to supplying us inwardly, God's Word

---

1. To help you cultivate this healthy habit, we suggest reading the devotional Daily Food, also available from this Publisher. Each volume of this devotional contains eight weeks of spiritual food, many Bible verses, and some practical guidance to help you advance daily in the Christian walk.

washes away our old and unbecoming thoughts. The apostle Paul told us in Ephesians 5:26 that, by "the washing of water by the Word," Christ cleanses away every blemish (stain of sin) and every wrinkle (sign of spiritual aging sign). As we read and pray the Word, we feel all the negative things within us being washed away.

In order to mature spiritually and have a life with inner quality, we must appreciate God's Word. When we turn the Bible into our prayer, we touch the Spirit within it – the life-giving Spirit (John 6:63). The more we do this, the more God's Word will abide in us, filling us with the divine life (John 5:39-40; Colossians 3:16). As opposed to some mental, intellectual exercise, this spiritual practice will help you mingle the Word with prayer; that is, with faith. Those who come to the Bible in this manner quickly gain wisdom and spiritual discernment.

Hebrews chapter 4 tells us that the Word of God is living and effective, sharper than any two-edged sword. As it cuts through, the Word performs a deep dividing work within us. It separates the things of the soul from those of the spirit, manifesting the thoughts and purposes of our heart, that we may not be deceived by them (v. 12). It is indispensable that we receive the Word with faith, ruminate it, consider it before God, mingle it with prayer, and apply it in our daily lives. This way, as we are infused by God's life, our impurities will be removed.

Today, our greatest need is to lay hold of God's Word with faith and practice it in our daily living. Otherwise, despite knowing many verses, we will remain as children who cannot be given solid food, which we need to carry out God's will (Hebrews 5:11-12). If we are to become mature sons, we need this relationship with God's Word. We must allow the Lord to touch, subdue, and transform our soul by His life.

The Importance of a Continuous and Daily Consecration

Consecrating ourselves to the Lord is another important step we must take. We must give Him our lives, future, as well as everything that we are and have. Consecration pertains to presenting ourselves before God as a living, holy, and acceptable sacrifice (Romans 12:1). We surrender and give ourselves to God, that He might change our position, usefulness, and destiny. Though we have our human activities (study, work, etc), our position has already been changed! In the past, we were in the world and of the world, but now we are in Christ; we are His!

We worked in the world and for the world, where we pursued our dreams and ideals, exhausting all our skills and abilities. Now, we have willingly surrendered ourselves to the Lord, that we may be useful to Him wherever we are. In other words, we are open for the

Lord to shape and mold us. In fact, the extent of our openness, our willingness, determines how useful we are to Him. When we consecrate ourselves to the Lord, our lives return to their original purpose – serving and cooperating with God to establish His will and kingdom here.

If this is our goal, we will no longer live a life for ourselves; that is, we will cease running after the wind and will no longer be as sheep without a shepherd (Ephesians 4:17; Matthew 9:36).

There are two important aspects to a solid and intense consecration: the first one pertains to having a solid foundation on which to consecrate ourselves. We must realize that, having been purchased by God, we must consecrate ourselves to Him, for we are His. The second aspect refers to having the right motivation: love. God poured out His love into our hearts, that we may consecrate ourselves to Him willingly.

1 Corinthians 6:20 reads, "For you were bought at a price." Our consecration is based on the fact that God purchased us. He paid a high price to satisfy His righteous requirements. When God purchased us with the precious blood His beloved Son shed on the cross, we became His. In other words, His blood provides Him ownership over us (1 Peter 1:18-19; 2:9), which means we no longer belong to ourselves. The Lord paid a high price to redeem us for Himself, which is why He expects us to consecrate ourselves to Him daily.

Throughout our lives, most of our consecration is motivated by feelings, which are unstable and volatile. Sometimes, after hearing or reading the Bible, we feel like consecrating ourselves. Then, if the feeling goes away the next day, we just forget about the whole thing. However, whether we feel happy or not, whether we feel like giving ourselves to the Lord or not, we must surrender ourselves to Him. Our consecration is based on God's purchase and rights over us.

Despite the fact our great God has every right over us, He wants to motivate us. Hence, He has poured out His love into our hearts, so our consecration is not out of obligation, but voluntary. He wants us to be prisoners of His love, servants who, having been freed, choose not to leave their Master (Exodus 21:2, 5). 2 Corinthians 5:14-15 reads, "For the love of Christ compels us... and He [Christ] died for all, that those who live should live no longer for themselves, but for Him who died for them and rose again."

The love of Christ floods our hearts, compelling us to consecrate ourselves and live for Him. It is because of love that we give God all that we are and have: our being, our future, our family, our material riches, and everything else. Such a consecration is sweet, beautiful, and ever new. God's great love and the high price He paid for us demonstrate how precious we are to Him. We can experience this great love heralded by the Word daily and everywhere.

Our consecration must be daily and unceasing. However, after giving ourselves to God, along with our future, time, family, and resources, we may end up taking back most of what we offered. When that happens, we feel disappointed in ourselves and even confused. While we may feel ashamed of approaching God, we must not be discouraged from turning back to Him. Satan uses this kind of discouraging feeling to keep us from returning to God and progressing in our consecration.

In the Old Testament, God commended that a burnt offering be made on a daily basis (Numbers 28:3-6). A lamb was offered in the morning, and another at dusk. Aware of our weaknesses, the Lord established daily offerings. If we only had one chance to consecrate ourselves to the Lord, and failed to do it, we would remain under His disapproval definitively. As a matter of fact, no one would be approved. We thank the Lord that we can renew our consecration and have a new beginning with Him daily.

Lamentations 3:22-23 reads, "Through the LORD's mercies we are not consumed, because His compassions fail not. They are new every morning; great is Your faithfulness." Though we may have failed many times in the past, each new day is a chance to have a new beginning with the Lord. When you wake up in the morning, thank the Lord and say, "Oh Lord Jesus, thank You for another morning. It is because of Your mercy that I can have a new beginning with You! I am Yours, Lord, and I want Your life to spread a little more in me today."

Suppose you have a good time of prayer and fellowship with the Lord in the morning. Then, as you go about your day, time goes by, many things happen, and you forget the consecrating prayer you made in the morning. If that should happen, fear not, for you can still offer up a "dusk burnt offering." Praise God! You can turn back to the Lord anytime, and He will enlighten you. In the Lord's light, you can repent, confess your sins, and renew your consecration. If you have this practice, you will enjoy good, peaceful nights of sleep. You can have a new beginning with the Lord every morning.

Confessing Our Sins

Whenever we consecrate ourselves to the Lord, we are enlightened by Him. Since God is light, our sins, impurities of the mind, and unbecoming behavior are inevitably exposed in His presence. At which time, you must confess everything to Him and lay hold of His precious blood. David said, "They looked to Him and were radiant" (Psalms 34:5). He also highlighted the following: "When I kept silent, my bones grew old, through my groaning all the day long. For day and night Your hand was heavy upon me; my vitality was turned into the drought of summer. I acknowledged my sin to You, and my iniquity I have not hidden. I said, 'I will confess my transgressions to the LORD,' And You forgave the iniquity of my sin" (32:3-5). Proverbs 28:13 reads, "He who covers his sins will not prosper; but whoever confesses and forsakes them will have mercy." To rid ourselves of all anxiety and inner dryness, we must always be willing to confess our sins. "If we confess our sins, He is faithful and just to forgive us our sins and to cleanse us from all unrighteousness" (1 John 1:9).

If we take advantage of every day, of every opportunity, confessing our failures and consecrating ourselves to the Lord anew, He will have a way to gain us completely, though some areas of our life may take a few years to overcome.

These continuous experiences will eventually make us absolute for the Lord. We will no longer live for ourselves, but for God and through God. The more the divine life grows in us, the more we can cooperate with the Lord in spreading His life to others. Only then will our lives have purpose and inner quality. God needs people He can count on to help bring His kingdom to earth.

Following the Lord Individually

The Lord is the Spirit today, and we must follow Him every day if we want to carry out His will and have a life with purpose and inner quality. According to the New Testament, we must walk in spirit and deny ourselves (Matthew 16:24-25; Galatians 5:16, 22-25). As we set our minds on the spirit, we enjoy life and peace (Romans 8:6). The more we turn our minds to the spirit, the more God's life grows in us.

Calling on the Lord's name and pray-reading His Word are practices taught by the apostles to help us turn to our spirit (John 6:63; 1 Corinthians 12:3). In order to remain in spirit, in fellowship with the Spirit, we must pray unceasingly and give thanks to God in all things (1 Thessalonians 5:17-18). We thank God that we can call on the Lord's name anytime and anywhere!

If you go a while without exercising your spirit, you may experience resistance when you get back to it. Without exercise, our spirit becomes deadened and stiff, much like an arm or a leg that have been in a cast for a long while. Once the cast is removed, multiple sessions of physical therapy – repetitive, continuous exercise – are often required to return the injured member to normalcy. Now the same can happen to our spirit, which is why we must keep it always exercised!

If we live in spirit and follow the Lord, we will seek His kingdom, His righteousness, and do as He commands (Matthew 6:25-34). Those who follow the Lord enjoy the certainty of His care, the blessing of not being anxious concerning eating, drinking, or clothing. As opposed to those who do not know God, we are free from the concerns associated with material things and making a living.

We live a life of following the Lord, calling on His name, eating His Word, having fellowship Him, consecrating ourselves to Him daily, exercising our spirit in prayer, and seeking His kingdom first. We can enjoy life and peace, for we are certain that our Father knows and meets our every need. We have this assurance because we know that the purpose of our lives is to do the will of our heavenly Father!

Following the Lord With Others

While some of us may have started out seeking the Lord on our own, we eventually felt a spontaneous desire to be with others who also followed Him (2 Timothy 2:22). In other words, we felt the need of meeting together as the church. When we received God's life, in addition to becoming His children, we became members of the Body of Christ (1 Corinthians 12:13). This latter aspect implies that we need one another for supply and perfecting as we exercise our function in the Body of Christ (Ephesians 4:12-16).

Now this supply is only found in the church meetings, where we can all exercise our function as members of the Body of Christ. All who have tasted the church life and spent time with the brethren testify it is one of the most genuine and comforting experiences of Christ's love among men (Psalm 133:1).

In his first epistle to the Corinthians, the apostle Paul says, "Now concerning spiritual gifts, brethren, I do not want you to be ignorant: You know that you were Gentiles, carried away to these dumb idols, however you were led" (12:1-2). Paul wanted them to appreciate the fact that, having believed in God, who is the Word, they had been empowered to open their mouths to call on the Lord's name and speak for Him; they were no longer dumb worshippers of dumb idols (1 Corinthians 12:3; 14:24, 31).

The more we exercise by calling on the Lord's name, the more we can manifest the gifts given to us by the Spirit. We must also exercise our gifts, so that our function in the Body is evidenced by the growth of God's life in us. This way, as each member functions according to their God-given measure, the Lord can carry out His will as Head of the Body (12:4-6).

The church is the Body of Christ, and we, the believers in Christ, are members of this Body: "Now you are the body of Christ, and members individually" (v. 27). As in our physical body, each one of us has a function as members of the Body of Christ. Working together and in cooperation, we, the many members, constitute one Body. Each member is important and indispensable. What a wonderful picture!

Love, The Most Excellent Way

After addressing the importance of every member of the Body of Christ, the apostle Paul reveals, in chapter 13, that love is the way to have a most excellent church life. Love is the expression of God's life, for He is love (1 John 4:8). How can we tell whether we are growing in the divine life? Not by our many works for the Lord, but by how much we love people. We express this love by preaching the gospel of grace[2] to our relatives, friends, and neighbors who have not yet received the Lord Jesus. We also express it by preaching the gospel of the kingdom[3] to believers whose spiritual growth has come to a halt. Those who love, shepherd and feed the Lord's sheep (John 21:15-17).

God has shown us that, our selfishness – thinking only of ourselves, seeking only our interests, worrying only about our needs, and caring exclusively for our own "spirituality" – will prevent us from having a life with inner quality. The Bible teaches us that those who deny themselves, care for the ones God placed under their care, and live by His will are blessed; that is, they are happy (Matthew 24:45-47). As the divine life grows in us, so does His nature, that we may express His love in our daily living. If we allow the Lord to gradually grow in us, our love for people will increase as we become more and more like Him: "By this we know love, because He laid down His life for us. And we also ought to lay down our lives for the brethren" (1 John 3:16).

---

2. The gospel of grace refers to the work carried out by the Lord, the good news, to deliver us from our sins and give us a new life. Christ did everything for us, and we must only believe it to receive His salvation into our spirit (John 3:3-5; 15-16; Ephesians 2:5-8).

3. The gospel of the kingdom refers to our need for the divine life we received to grow in us. In order for that to happen, we must deny our self daily, so that God's life can grow and mature within us. Our growth will qualify us to reign with the Lord in the coming age. This aspect of our salvation is our responsibility, as it depends on our willingness and cooperation to reach the end of our faith, the salvation of our soul (Matthew 16:24-25; 1 Peter 1:9).

This is the meaning of our life! Let us always be mindful that God created us to cooperate with Him. God's original commission to Adam has been given to us, His children – to be fruitful, multiply, fill the earth with the divine life, subdue it by means of His authority, usher in His kingdom, and defeat His enemy (Genesis 1:28, Hebrews 2:5-9). God's full salvation begins when He pours His life into our spirit. After that, it continues as His life seeps in and permeates our soul. In the end, even our body will be transformed and glorified by His life (Philippians 3:21). This salvation cannot stop in us, but should flow from us as rivers of living water to reach others (John 7:38).

Now that we can see God's will and purpose in creating man, our hearts must be enlarged. In addition to enjoying the Lord's presence daily, consecrating ourselves to Him, calling on His name, reading and praying His Word, we must take care of those around us. If we preach the gospel and have a heart to shepherd people, we will share the divine life with everyone, everywhere – our relatives, coworkers, fellow students, friends, neighbors, etc. This is the way to practice what the Lord Jesus said in the gospel of Mark, "And you shall love the LORD your God with all your heart, with all your soul, with all your mind, and with all your strength... and you shall love your neighbor as yourself" (12:30-31). This will assure us, and those around us, a life with purpose and inner quality.

Let us pray, "*I want to worship You, Lord Jesus! Even though I am a sinner, You came to save me and give me a new beginning. Lord, thank You for Your wonderful and complete salvation! Please, forgive me for my selfish ways, thinking only of myself and my own desires. Lord, I want to consecrate myself to You, so Your life can conquer and saturate every part of my being. Deliver me from all stagnation, I want to grow and follow You every single day of my life! Help me call on Your precious name, eat of Your Word, and exercise my spirit more! Oh Lord Jesus!*

My Lord Jesus! I love calling on Your name! Help me grow with and appreciate the function of my brethren in the church. Help me be faithful in using the gifts You have given me, so my life is useful in Your hands. Lord Jesus, I pray that Your life within me may flow out and reach those around me, so they may feel Your love and follow You. Lord, I want to grow in life, do Your will, share Your life with everyone, bring Your kingdom to earth, and help defeat Your enemy here. Jesus is Lord!"